Wind in the Elephant Tree

Earl Vincent de Berge

ISBN: 978-81-963161-1-2

First Edition: 2023
Rs. 200/-

Cyberwit.net
HIG 45 Kaushambi Kunj, Kalindipuram
Allahabad - 211011 (U.P.) India
http://www.cyberwit.net
Tel: +(91) 9415091004
E-mail: info@cyberwit.net

Printed at QUARTERFOLD PRINTABILITIES.

INTRODUCTION: About These Poems

The book title, *Wind in the Elephant Tree*, traces to a time when, at age 20, I rough-necked my way through wilderness deserts of Mexico with several friends. I came to realize that although I was strong, reasonably good-looking and becoming well educated, I could perish in the desert and no one would care except ants, vultures and maybe my younger sister. The realization that neither I, nor anyone else, is the center of the universe has never faded.

Elephant trees in bloom

The elephant tree is a stout, scantily-foliaged desert survivor whose bark smells faintly of turpentine. It makes lovely small pink flowers after rain and is often found standing alone, or in widely dispersed clusters, each tree silently observing life and death struggles in the desert that is its Spartan world. Little but hot wind passes through its branches. I concluded that if such a plain desert tree can survive and still be a vision of rugged beauty, I could embrace it as an icon of my belief that beauty is everywhere if I just give it a chance to enter my consciousness.

At about the same time, I began a journey to find the meaning of love in my life — a search triggered by watching my parents wage a bitter struggle to hurt each other, using their children as pawns. They were still at it when I turned 50. Most of the poems selected for this volume are love poems or valentines to Suzanne, my life partner; we met in college and married just after she graduated. Other poems reflect candidly on my college roller-coaster years seeking friendships, sex, love and a woman I could love and trust and who felt that way about me. Writing poems helped me sort through my thoughts and experiences as I sought to identify what values in love, friendship, and society were meaningful to me.

At age 15, my brain and emotions were freed from the tensions in my birth family when I was enrolled in an excellent, remote college-prep boarding school located in the mountains of northern Arizona. It had a strong cross-cultural curriculum and an ethnically-mixed student body and faculty from all over the world. I came to value cultural diversity and to question the opinions of my parents.

When I advanced to college in Ohio (and on-campus dormitory life) my understanding of and respect for the goals and limitations of others, and of myself, accelerated. Through poetry I discovered that I am an optimist, humanist, empiricist and romantic, with a powerful interest in music, government, and the natural world. Fellow scholars and experiences filled my head with new ways of thinking and I developed a life-long thirst for learning. And that was good enough, until women and hormones demanded space in my brain. Women confused me and I determined to become unconfused.

College women tutored me about honesty in adult relationships and how to distinguish between lust, fascination, trust and love. At first, I focused on lust and had a jolly time as college women advanced my education from curiosity and lustful experimentation to unrealistic expectations, confusion and finally to love. College also helped me find the woman I married, who has been my joy for six decades. My life with her is expressed in this book.

LOVE IS

Losing one's mind and not
searching to regain it.

Believing that the one you love
is uniquely exquisite.

Finding a new language and
someone to speak it with.

Contents

Chapter 1 – Decades of Honeymoon

DECADES OF HONEYMOON

I met Suzanne in my final year of undergraduate studies at Antioch College in Ohio. She was a third-year fine arts major from Minneapolis, liberal-leaning and smart as hell. Pretty, with calm hazel eyes, Suzanne was a sculptor in metal, stone and wood; a horseman; and was adventurous. I fell in love.

When she told me she loved me too, I proposed, she accepted and we were married a year later in Minneapolis, after she graduated. During the interval, I was in Tucson working on my Masters degree in Political Science. We honeymooned in the Rocky Mountains and northern Arizona on our 'way to Tucson where I continued in graduate school. I had not met her family until we were married; they turned out to be wonderful people.

Suzanne in Jerome, AZ

The following chapter contains some of the love letters, valentines, and birthday poems I wrote to Suzanne over the years.

SUZANNE BEGUILES ME

To me, it is the richness and
kindness of your mind
that beguiles my intellect.

From your caring, tender touch,
my heart grasps the fullness
of your grace and beauty.

The two combined
are a greater gift
than I deserve.

Tucson 1965

Suzanne in El Salvador

ALL THE WAY

Questing for honest love in these college days,
please accept my earnest lover's praise
and ignore suitors from the milling herd
whispering promises quite absurd.

Be not coy with me nor proud,
cut me out from that silly crowd
for when the blush of our youth flies away
I'll still be at your side, all the way.

Tucson 1964

I WOULD SEND YOU A LETTER

I would send you a letter of my love,
my love, but no postman has ever
heard of this place and no postbox
can be found among the cacti.

I will send you a letter of my love,
my love, carried on the winds with
birds and gentle fragrances of
of sensuous night-blooming flowers.

I will send you a love letter, my love,
in the songs of coyotes singing
on the knoll and of mountain lions
roaring lustily up the canyon.

I will send you a letter of my love,
my love, through the songs of doves
and orioles as they coo and twitter
happily among eccentric desert trees.

I will send you a letter of my love,
my love, through the stars that canopy
our lives and on a warm evening
breeze to tousle your hair.

Scammon's Lagoon, Mexico

WERE I A COMPOSER

Were I a composer I would compose
for you bright and soft songs about
natural voices in virgin deserts.

I'd score the lilting sounds
of a tranquil land that gives its all
and asks for nothing in return.

You would hear the voices of light
winds when mourning doves
begin their coo-coo-curoo

and quail and lady cactus wrens
hail dawn with calls of humor and
glee that foraging time has returned.

There would be soft night songs
of owls hooting and the low rumble
of a mountain lion calling for love.

You will hear rabbits scurrying at your
approach and if you listen closely,
a cricket song in the distance.

It will be gentle music you
will be happy to receive
and in return, disturb nothing.

1964 Baja California, Mexico

SELECTED VALENTINES FROM OVER THE DECADES

After dawn I walk this cactus land
thinking of O'Keefe's lush flowers.
I seek to photograph the immodest
blooms of a prickly hedgehog cactus
hunkered unassuming on the sand.

I find one in bloom, its tiny flowers
and velvet petals face the world
in such hopeful soft tranquility.
I think of your festive eyes and face,
for you like they, are an essence of grace. (1965)

~

I have been alone, singing solo
on a road surrounded by a scramble
of wildflowers and weeds, where singing solo
always brought me a good but simple tune.
Then I discovered the joy of quietly
singing in harmony with you. (1966)

~

Feathers of twilight edge into our room
and rest on the sheet of linen drawn
gently to conceal your languid form.
Abstraction does not rob your
beauty — the inviting forms
enhance your mysterious nature

and sparks this observer to seek
more of what lies beneath the veil.   (1967)

~

I am made whole when
among its many treasures
nature offers for my quiet regard
a lavender Iris along the path
or, in the gentle light of dawn,
your peaceful sleeping face,
and I wonder of what you dream.   (1978)

~

I despair being unable to convey
to you in a simple poem, that I still
walk among the flowers lining golden
grain fields of our younger days. It is
a path that reflects my dreams and
passions and the sharing we still do.   (1998)

~

As the great aircraft rises
above the desert floor
into rose-tipped clouds
of the dawning sun,
my heart lies asleep, her hip-
length hair spread
across yellow pillows
framing her peaceful face.   (2000)

~

Rare, free spirit, Suzanne you are my dawn!
Near, you are a gift that brings a warm wind.
Bust, lust, warm cuddling, farm, pool, dusk.
Rise, flow, soar, enjoy with me, for if we could fly,
our air would be champagne, bubbling, effervescent,
every glass higher than the last.   (2003)

Each night for these so many years
you dream smiling next to me, content,
warm, immersed in slumber's grace.
Thank you my sweet daffodil
for each creamy thrill. (2005)

~

Sunset's golden beams
alight silently on my arms
as might a butterfly on flowers.
The hair in feverish glow
welcomes thoughts of you
sitting calmly by candlelight. (2006)

~

I love you even more than yesterday
which was a banner day itself —
so when you slide home let's play
and put our watches on the shelf. (2014)

~

Our love for one another
and the care to each we give
is the energy that gives us life. (2017)

~

I fancy you as a gentle summer cloud
floating, cruising, and transforming
the splendid firmament of our lives.
You are to me a fine complex red wine,
so let's have a merry time on this ridge
above the Copan ruins where millennia
of lovers have delighted at nature's beauty
and sighed happily in the love they share.

On our 47th Anniversary, Copan Honduras

HONEYMOON

Sleeping beside me as we cross the prairie,
your soft breathing calms me as I reflect
that I am no longer a lone individual but now
with a life partner to whom I am fully responsible.
Chromatic sunset melds my heart with hers.

Later, a nudge brings her warm thigh
close as sleepy lips caress my neck
and skilled kind hands comfort my back
until slumber relaxes love's fondle
as we both slide back into sleep.

I love you Suzanne mine,
you have won my small worth.
Sleep gently at my happy side
and awaken calm, tender and secure.

On our honeymoon we enjoyed
the northern great plains, camped
in Yellowstone and at Navajo Mountain
trading post, paused in Walnut and Grand
canyons, Painted Desert, Meteor Creator,
slept in a teepee on your rich uncle's
ranch in Montana, explored Four Corners
canyon country and then descended into
Sonoran desert where we expanded
our love for each other and nature.

Our love is in the things we seek,
passion warms the love we share.

1965

Suzanne in Tucson 1966

MESSENGERS

Fluffy white clouds
        seem within my reach.
Are they messengers of your love,
        soft, gently churning,
in such warm colors sent
        to comfort my soul?
A glorious flower opened
        in the night
now radiant with the dawn.

1964 Tucson

DAWN'S FINGERS

Blue-tipped fingers of dawn
pull me willingly into her sleepy
embrace, warm breathing on my cheek
and little sounds that may be words.

But for her, I might like my father be:
hard, gloating on the faults of others,
sequestered against debate; unforgiving,
afraid of trial and in the end, alone.

From her come open eyes and heart
caring for those who seek knowledge
for itself, putting false pride behind
... making us better for each other.

FALLING ASLEEP

I cup your breast as we lie cradled,
your back and soft rump warm
against me. Drifting toward sleep
all is silent except for soft breathing.

Sliding my hand to rest on your hip,
you make a small dove-like sound
expressing desire, until relaxing my hand
I urge: "Sleep, it's time to dream."

I watch kaleidoscopic colors and shapes
on the screen of my closed eyelids ...
strange patterns of retina sensors
firing dimly as they too fade into sleep.

Hawaii

NO NEED TO HURRY

Let it be early!
There is no need to hurry
while the nightingale
sings down the moon,
for we have plenty of time
to caress yet twice again.

Ignore the rising sun.
Enjoy our gift of sleepy lips
and practiced fingertips.
We require no change of pace
pull the covers up once more,
it's time to drift without a care.

Ubeda, Spain

WHO CARES?

Through our bedroom curtains
dawn spreads its warm yellow glow
as after deep sleep and dreams we are
ushered to some ambrosial place
to enjoy the depths of each other's
flesh and passion for pleasure.
Who cares about the sunrise?

Jerome, AZ

WISHING

As spring's green lace unfolds,
a misty rain drifts down the slopes
and across our awakening world
to where I sit, quietly wishing
your hand would find mine.

2004

TO ME YOU ARE

A song on the breeze.
A slice of mango on my tongue.
Lips' welcome greeting.
Seven silver bells on the air.

A stone skipping across a tranquil lake.
The sound of muted voices talking slowly.
Your breath on my temple.
A comforting whisper in the night.

Your smile, a kiss on my eyes,
the caress of mist from a cloud.
A draft of cool water in summer
With your name — profound sleep.

2007 Copan, Honduras

LIGHTS MY WAY

Elegant and evocative
in chestnut with grey,
your hair still falls
in its alluring way.

Aromas of soil and plants
touch your hair by day ...
At night a citrus scent
in after-shower glow.

Genteel hair piled high
is somehow witch-crafted
around your fetching face
to light my way into your arms.

2015

HOW THINGS CHANGE SO LITTLE

Only yesterday I longed to be
cloaked in nothing but your voice,
love, and low-toned chuckles.

It is the same today as then,
but I also appreciate a warm
sweater and sheepskin slippers.

2013

WHEN YOU LOOK AT ME

I see in your smile how you taught me
to enjoy the pastels of cactus blossoms
in soft morning light —

to be gladdened watching a bee, butterfly
or ant doing their business
among flowers.

How a tiny cactus flower flutters its colorful plea
to attract just the right pollinators and
how each gives as well as receives.

The twitching paws of a sleeping dog
who finally calmed that itch
and now dreams of chasing our cat.

2000

Chapter 2 – In Her Gardens

IN HER GARDENS

Suzanne with flowers in Antigua

Suzanne's love for animals is paired with her joy in nurturing flowering and food-producing plants and trees, which she has done everywhere we have lived — from our small urban farm in the Arizona desert to the tropics of Guatemala, where she added orchids, bromeliads and avocados to her palette, and then again in the mountains of Arizona.

I have written elsewhere of her work in Guatemala spanning two decades. Her NGO, Seeds for a Future, is successful and has been well-received by more than 2,200 poor rural families in 20+ rural communities. It continues to expand as it offers training in how to ensure better nutrition for children and other family members through "backyard farms" where they grow vegetables and raise small protein animals such as rabbits and poultry. But it was on our little farm in Phoenix that I came to see her love for both plants and animals.

Suzanne on our farm

THE PLACE WE BOTH NEED TO BE

Nothing is finer than watching Suzanne in June
gardening where earth and sky are her cocoon.
Above her, a thrasher pair each take their turn
sitting tiny eggs, their main concern.

Around the vintage house on our small urban farm,
hundreds of flowers open, each a sun-filled chalice
and the new seeds she sews will soon ignite
as nature's wonders seek warm sunlight.

The air is hot and our skin soon glistens,
as to nature's heart we gladly listen.
This haven is surely of she and me
— it is the place we both need be.

2010 Phoenix

A GOOD DAY

Closing the rabbit-proof gate
    of her vegetable garden
Suzanne gazes back briefly
    to admire the healthy
colors and odors of plants and soil.

Eight radishes in hand,
    she crosses the gravel drive
as the gay crunch of stones
    sounds like an invitation
to the rest of a good day.

2004 Phoenix

CUTTING ROSES

Early on an Arizona spring day
Suzanne is singing softly, cutting
roses along the pasture fence.
At her side, an old wicker basket
overflows with red and yellow flowers
from those we planted over the years.
Listening to birds singing in the olive tree
and to the quiet snoring of aging dog Hue-Hue
at her side, she is wholly within herself.

2006 Phoenix

PLANTING IRIS

Our world is music and we
the players of gentle notes
rising through our hands
as we plant iris and daffodil
bulbs in soft black volcanic soil.
Mellow music flows into my arms,
in harmony with the soil for giving
bulbs an opportunity to flourish.

Working quietly beside me,
your fingers massage the loam,
deftly marrying bulbs and soil –
babies and womb — which ask
only for water and warmth
to become a brilliant celestial song
pulsing in our tiny universe.

2010 Antigua, Guatemala

LOVED ONE SINGING

In earlier times, music garnished
a bucolic world on relaxed occasions
filling moments with familiar tuneful
creations to calm or cheer the soul.

In modern times, noise extinguishes silence
so totally, so brutally, and so continuously
that when it pauses, pressures on my mind
are released into a tabernacle of serenity.

To hear my loved one singing softly
to herself in the garden reminds me
of the beauty of quietude and of the
comfort and peace of mind music brings.

2002

GARDEN BUDDAHS

Fetching garden ornaments,
    soft-hearted to their core,
yellow pear-shaped tomatoes
    hang plump in summer air
swollen with pride, pleasantly
    lulled to maturity by warm
days and gardener's tender care.

Each awaits Suzanne's hand to
    gently check its health,
blissfully unaware its maturity
    is its demise for a salad
or consumption on the spot.

2009 Phoenix

TWO VOICES

Returning from her herb garden
Suzanne opens the kitchen door
beside the blue wooden table built
to set things on when entering.

Not hearing the door close, I know
she has paused to visit our aging cat
Raya who camps on the table within
reach of loving hands and kitty treats.

Suzanne rubs Raya's jowls, asks
a rhetorical question about her day
as Raya's low purr, a subtle semaphore,
avows pleasure and their trusted bond

2005 Phoenix

HIGH UPON YOUR NECK

Sitting beside fragrant four o'clocks,
a well-formed casual knot of braided hair
lies high upon your neck as you cast
graceful thoughts and smiles upon
the welcome late afternoon breeze.

1999 Phoenix

FLEETING SHADE

Hiking South Mountain on Sundays,
Suzanne leads on sure legs and undulating hips.
I follow for the healthy things climbing does
and the visual delight she effortlessly provides.

Trail-side stones have no interest in why
we plod the desert amidst their flat or jagged
countenance. Ants work tirelessly in their tasks,
facing endless barriers that define their world.

Oblivious to everything but their tasks, ants
simply are. We loom as gigantic animations in
the searing heat, offering only a fleeting shade
that passes quickly — like clouds.

2006

THANKSGIVING

As late afternoon sunlight
sculpts cactus and trees
to their gentlest forms,
our feast has been consumed,
so we leisurely stroll arm-in-arm
amidst neighborly hails as we speak
quietly about warm memories
of family and friends gathered
over years past for a bounty
beyond the food and wine.

2012 Phoenix

WHERE WE ONCE GRAZED

We sheltered in this harbor four decades,
this sanctuary of house and pastureland
– so peaceful, tranquil and nurturing.

We think of it as ours alone, yet it is hospice
to hundreds: quail and hawks, thrashers,
cardinals, gophers and rabbits, hens, pet
lovebirds and parrots gone feral, ducks,
turkeys, horses and colts, ewes and their lambs,
prowling coyotes sniffing for careless chickens,
doves by the dozen, ravens, sandpipers and
killdeer crying while our dogs patrol parameters,
willing to bite or wag depending on your scent.

But now that we must go, I feel as the ewes
and do not want to look up from where we
happily grazed so long and so content.
I will sorely miss lambing season.

2015

Chapter 3 – Our Guatemala and Latin America Years

Our Guatemala and Latin America Years

From our first days together, we made learning more about the people and history of Latin America and the cultural history of pre-Columbian peoples a major part of our lives. We started in Mexico and its amazing cultural and recreational opportunities ranging from the deserts and remote beaches of Baja California to verdant Isla Mujeres in the Yucatan, to major urban areas of Mexico City, Guadalajara, and Monterrey.

Some of our most interesting experiences were in Honduras, Peru, El Salvador and Ecuador, and especially in Guatemala where we worked on archaeological sites and invested in a second home from which we explored Central America.

Guatemala is a beautiful country filled with amicable and creative people whose breath-taking arts, culture and history trace back to impressive pre-Columbian civilizations, principally the Maya, and to the Spanish "conquest." When we first visited, Guatemala was struggling with a nasty, decades-long civil war that pitted rich against poor, indigenous people against families of European descent (mostly German and Spanish), as well as complex tensions between Catholicism, Christian fundamentalism, and the strongly lingering belief systems of modern Maya people.

Guatemala and its people are dear to us and I have written much about what I saw and assessed during those years. But Guatemala is also a place where we had time to dig deeper into why we loved each other.

PAUSE FOR THOUGHT

I have developed multiple loves
and admit careening between them
in pursuit of joy, security, kindness
and self-understanding. At the heart
of my search has been you, Suzanne,
a most singular woman and heart.

My other loves are writing poetry, politics
and street photography — all help feed
my restless, searching mind with reality
and help my intellect accept the many harsh,
obscure truths hidden in the pretenses
of society, government, business and religion.

Our travels in Latin America and your sober
observations ever give me pause for thought.

2020 Antigua

ALL THAT WE NEED

Dimming in glow, the moon
slowly gains speed toward
night's horizon, then winks
and slides behind mountains,
leaving starry sky to lovers.

Tipsy Mariachis entertain
at a wedding in our village
amidst tall corn milpas
sprawling on volcanic hillsides.
Happiness gathers steam.

Kissing spreads as drunk musicians
move closer and we marvel
they can stay upright with
their eyes closed, feet a-tapping
and fingers strumming.

On this balmy tropical evening
we stargazers with a penchant for
comets, eclipses and pastel sun rises
confess that being hand-in-hand
is all the Valentine we need.

2009 Quetzaltenango

ASCENDING FLOWER

Floating skyward to our upper patio
on an ancient stone staircase festooned
with morning glories, Suzanne ascends
for sun's morning warmth in her soft vintage
coral sweater and pale yellow scarf.

Teacup in hand, wisps of hair
flutter gently against cheek and neck
where she pauses to inspect the
passion vine, sniff a full open flower
and pinch off yellowing leaves.

2013 Antigua

LUCKY CHAP

I am a lucky chap ...
Nests in two countries
each with a quiet writing office
giving a clear-air view of
nature, gardens, mountains,
wildlife, vast skies, clouds,
In one, an active volcano daily
sculpts our world, coughing
new gas and rock.
Never the same.
Never sorrowful.
The only things better than these
are the calm of a long marriage
and the understanding it brings.

2016
On Suzanne's 73rd birthday

Together in Guatemala

EXPIRATION DATE

Obscure to its fabricators,
love's expiration date
earns extended life
via respect and awareness.

It is recalibrated daily
on the borders of
self-definition and how each
defines "I" and "We."

Enduring love is about resisting
the "we are one" fallacy.
We cannot be "we" while focused on "I",
nor be "I" while focused on "we."

The enduring two must retain
their essential "I" while seeking
not to become the other,
nor that the other become them.

2010

LAUGHING AT ME

I sigh perceptibly
as you lean forward
in your unfastened blouse,
the upper two-thirds
of your breasts laughing
at me above your
curving inner neckline,
inviting gentle lust that
will be accepted,
but not just now,
for a frappuchino
is in your hand as we sit
beneath park trees
festooned with lavender blossoms
while a Sunday circus of
humanity strolls past.

2002 Xela, Guatemala

BEFORE

Before this agitated, brimming brain
is drained of poems by my nomadic pen

and before I tire of gazing upon your
mature smile and into your hazel eyes,

love itself would have to lose all
of its strange powers.

2006

MORNING SUNLIGHT

On the black volcanic slopes above the waters
of storied Lake Atitlan, morning sunlight enlivens
the green leaves of coffee and cacao plants
until they look like lace draped casually over
the shoulders of an elegant, proud Black woman.

A light fog pours gently from clouds over her ebony
shoulders and arms, pausing only briefly on her breasts
to contemplate the waywardness of love before sliding
gently, cautiously, and hopefully toward the warm
waters of the lake of dancing light.

2004 Guatemala

THE VERY THOUGHT OF YOU

People-watching in the central square,
I drift into daydream — so many stimuli!
Daydreams of how my love for you grows,
deepens and better understands itself.

The animated images and smiling faces
of people relaxing in the park trigger
thoughts of your liberal open-heart:

- the chant of a woman marching for equal rights
- the swinging of your body as Billie Holiday sings
the very thought of you...
- your instincts grounded in trust of reason
- how you soar on the thermals of your humanity
- your sad sighs over newspaper stories of war and cruelty
- and why snack food makers sell early death.
- why so many Republicans seem devoid of compassion.

I daydreamt you were a Jacaranda flower
and I a well-mannered hummingbird.

2012 Antigua

YOU PRESS BACK TO SAY

Known and loved by me,
your arm and gentle hand,
the skin no longer so young
yet soft as romance itself,
rest across the *Prensa Libre*
as we read headlines together
of today's events in Guatemala.

The smiling waitress asks "Algo mas?"
and as one we murmur "No, gracias."
As I trace my fingers, not so absently
over your hand, one finger slides
between two. You press back to say
"I love you too," with skin I know so well.

Aug 2010 Birthday card

MORE THAN FAIR

Beneath a waning three-quarter moon,
el Volcan Fuego is a vague silhouette
in a hazy horizon. Fog snuffs west-moving stars
one by one. No winds stir where I sit.

Short strings of firefly lights birth and die.
and nearby with a low sweet tone
a good old dog says he'd like a bone.

I rise from an old wicker chair
in darkness to find my way to the
woman who knows my every fault
yet somehow still thinks sweetly of me.

She murmurs in her gentle way
she'll love me even as I lose my hair.
After 50 years, that's more than fair.

2014 Antigua

ON PENDING RETIREMENT

No longer to boss or clock be slave
nor any who require that I behave.

For food I'll breathe the blossomed air
and hang around with she who's fair.

We'll visit my desert's lost lagoon,
where hand-in-hand we'll watch the moon.

2005 Xela

IN MUTED WAYS

Petite yellow flower petals
nestled beside a blue sage bush
caught my eye some 50 years ago
and still draw me among photo
memories of our early years.
Its species name is unknown to me
unless *cherubic buttercup* will do.

Singled out in its lonely distinction —
pure yellow against grey green leaves —
it kindles memories of tranquility
although the tender dear will soon dry
and its color evaporate … *Se fue!*
Perhaps a seed or two survived.
Life goes on in muted ways.

2016

DRIFTING AWAY

On my peaceful path toward oblivion,
passions urge me to express admiration
for those who struggle against injustice
foisted upon on them by the unrelenting
greed of government, business, laws,
lawyers, racism and religion.

Increasingly I try to focus my spiritual core
on three beautiful and enduring aspects of my
life that lie at the center of who I have become.
I focus first, and daily, on Suzanne,
my closest, level-headed and trusted
companion in all things that we must face.
She is my Swiss compass on kindness,
humanism and demand for fair play.

My two other passions are writing poetry
and street photography — both help direct
my intellect to recognize humanism, pretense
and the often-harsh realities of life among humans.

Lust once played a distracting role
in my search to find my spiritual core
but that is drifting away with age.

2020 Prescott

BORN IN SUNRISE

Rising from the sea's dreamy embrace,
emerging in sunrise and salt-fragrant air,
she strolls upon the sand-- her blossoming
life sculpting small footprints on the sand.

Tan wet skin shines with droplets
of rainbows sliding down her smooth
arms and thighs, each burning fantasies
into the springtime of my far too eager eyes.

Baja Pacific coast 1973
and Sipacate, Guatemala 1998

ANOTHER VIEW OF GUATEMALA

We worked for a time as volunteers on an archaeological site in the small village of Chocolá, which lies on the western slope of the impressive volcano San Pedro. This experience gave me a personal insight into how people can come to manage and love life in a tropical environment, which I tried to relate in the poem “El Bosque” (The Forest).

EL BOSQUE

In those days I came to love
the rainforest's spread of emerald
lace above its tranquil forest floor

and the beams of sunlight igniting
flashing colors of butterfly wings
and silk strands of yellow caterpillars

descending for lunch amidst the rich
aromas of coffee plants, orchids
and volcanic soil – such a fertile world!

Late afternoon tropical rains begin
and farm workers cut palm fronds,
twist fibers into twine to bind nine sticks

gathered from the forest carpet to form
a waist-high ephemeral lean-to shelter
as the mother of rain pounds the fronds.

They motion us in with waves and smiles
where we six sit quietly, smoke weed,
chat and listen to nature's music.

Chocolá, Guatemala

Our experiences in Chocolá and elsewhere in rural Guatemala spanned three decades and gave us a closer view of the challenges and deprivation faced by people in rural Guatemala, and particularly by indigenous peoples. We came to more clearly understand that while Guatemala is beautiful geographically and culturally, it is also a country of great suffering, especially among its rural populations, who are at the bottom of the socio-economic ladder in so many ways that it can be difficult to understand their generally genial personalities. Malnutrition is chronic among mothers and children, and rural people suffer unemployment, under-employment, low income, poor education and limited access to health care. Municipal services are often minimal and plagued by favoritism. Criminal terrorism is a black snake ever coiled at their feet.

GUATEMALA NIGHTMARE

In pre-Columbian times, Maya people
revered land, corn and bean as gods' gifts,
fearing only that when Lord jaguar sneezed,
volcanos would roar, drought would come
and priests would sacrifice more virgins.

Today, modern government leaders demand
obedience for security and set aside justice,
liberty and peaceful discourse among equals.
Their armies shoot men in their fields and villages.

Next come drug lords, street gangs, extortionists,
corrupt police and elected officials. And more men
with machine guns, grenades and bayonets.
Both peace and security become mere fantasy.

Already staggering, indigenous cultures suffocate
beneath their growing numbers, poverty, prejudice, neglect
poor food security, and minimal health care.
Evangelicals challenge their belief in ancient gods.

> Do modern Maya long for earlier days
> when their fears centered on drought,
> disease or volcanic eruptions when
> their Lord Jaguar had slept poorly?

Suzanne and I asked ourselves what we might be able to do to help at least some rural Guatemalans live healthier lives. Beginning in 2007, planning and groundwork led us to create a non-profit (www.SeedsforaFuture.org) to provide women with training in home food production, along with education on nutrition and clean kitchen and food handling practices We were cautioned by "experts" that husbands would frown on their wives seeking such education outside the home. However, we found that by bringing our training directly into homes and neighborhoods and encouraging husbands to participate, we could accommodate the eagerness of women to learn new skills to improve their lives and the lives of their families. As of this writing, more than 2,400 families across 15 villages have completed a 12-month training program in nutrition gardens and raising small animals. When male family members realized they and their families were eating and feeling better, many social barriers fell away and demand for the program gained steam across the region.

Moms Arrive at Nutrition Seminar

Three Moms Show off Nutritious Herbs from their Gardens

Moms and daughters attend Cooking for Nutrition class in El Triunfo

Suzanne celebrates "Service to Humanity Award"
with Earl and lifelong friend Mark Winheld

Chapter 4 – Retirement

RETIREMENT YEARS

Our "retirement" refers to those years when we eased away from corporate matters and moved to residential living in the mountains of Arizona and Guatemala where we could reflect on the nature of nature and human development and where we could give sway to our artistic and humanitarian impulses. It is a wonderful time, but inevitably aging stuck its nose into our lives and rendered me homebound and Suzanne my "caregiver." She must have better "aging genes" than do I, for she has remained sturdier and healthier, and happily for me, caring and intellectually adventurous. Her father made it to 103 years and was a journalist warrior for justice and peace all the way. Suzanne is made of the same stuff.

These poems reflect some of my thoughts in those years. I should mention that at about 80 years of age, my "damn the torpedoes" bravado was muffled when Parkinson's, a neurological disease, pulled back on my reins. Then spinal stenosis jumped in, followed by a bad fall that gave me a compression fracture in a vertebrae and introduced me to the reality of relentless pain and loss of mobility.

But I am still kicking, so just let me say — it takes time to adjust. But it still is a joy to share my time on this fabulous planet with Suzanne.

ONE PATH

One path to a long happy
marriage lies in respecting each
fragment of the person you love,

rather than seeking to love
the undivided person. That is
too confusing, too demanding.

Find and love the fragments,
for there are many, and thus,
always much to love at all times.

2015 Antigua

FINGER OUR WINDOWS

Outside, wind-aroused branches
finger our windows
seeking more tranquil friends.

Inside, candles spread warm
calm yellow light
without murmur.

Asleep, your smile and wild hair on pillow
suggest flights of fanciful dreams
amid the calm of home and love.

2015 Antigua

DELIGHTS OF NOW

That which you wished for
I wished for as well,
and with delight we brimmed
our world each day.

That which I longed for
you longed for too,
and unshaken over the years,
found love is its own eternity.

Never served up cold or dry
we feasted on the delights
of now, chasing off wearisome.
contemplations of age.

Nature's parlor doors stand
open everywhere.
The fragrance of spring flowers
still makes us drunk.

2016 Antigua

MY WORLD IS BEST

My world is best when
among its many offerings
I pause to enjoy a lavender iris
or curl to you asleep at dawn.

And though our hair grows grey
and our steps shorten and slow,
your heart and spirit stay
entwined with mine.

1999

BEYOND MERE DREAMS

Retired now, our days flow amber-lush
amongst mountain daffodils and roses.

Quiet hours we meander hand-in-hand
as your love guides me beyond mere dreams.

Though I cannot fully grasp your emotions
nor sooth away all your latent fears,

I can understand and welcome
the calm your spirit ever seeds in me.

2013 Antigua

AT 54 YEARS

Our years in concert sum to 54
 and so very much more.
It is not sappy to say once more
 that I love you to your core

When I found you,
 I knew just what to do
and so, thank goodness, did you,
 as away west we flew.

Hot blood still races
 through our veins
although in recent times
 the pace is more relaxed
for we are in no hurry
 to reach the finish line.

2012 Houston

LOVE OF INNOCENCE

As the South Mountain range brightens
under the robust path of sunrise,
dark shadows on its wrinkled skin
warm from purple to lavender then gold.

The drama of sunrise ignites my respect
and love for you, expands my reality
from slumber's pace of indistinct dreams
to the charity of your love of innocence and justice
that ever shines in your eyes and deeds.

2010 Phoenix

SLEEP

Beneath the weight of nervous tension,
the torture of being neither asleep nor awake
yields thoughts akin to hallucinations,
fleeting into and beyond fragmented puzzles.

I wish only for the shelter of affection
in my wife's reassuring arms, that I may
sleep the night through as water unseen
in the bottom of a slow-meandering stream.

2002 Phoenix

MORNING RHYTHM

Head of bed slightly raised, and
glass skylight located so I can
watch the dawn each morning,
I quietly stretch old muscles
that ache whether I exercise or not
as I listen to her calm breathing.

Although longing for sex, I know
sleep is a gift as sweet as loving.
So I lie still, doze, hold her gently
when she stirs, talk quietly,
watch her dress and then rise.

2010

ESSENCE OF BUTTERFLY

Before, during and after
    we grew gray,
I pressed my lips to yours,
    lips that express our
passions and friendship.

Essence of butterfly —
    your spirit dances
upon ripening prairie wheat
    accompanied by
the joyous music you hum.

2008

WHAT MATTERED

What mattered when we first retired,
was to have no agenda and to relax
on the shores of love-inspiring lake Atitlan,
buy a shore-side house, a small boat
and name it "Lancha Suzanna."

Our two-story Spanish-style retreat had
a grand lake view and a floating
boat dock at its foot. Our blue lancha,
had good power, no leaks and a canopy
against tropical sun and rain.

Lancha Suzanna ferried us to markets and
stylish eateries in historic lakeshore towns
offering haute cuisine amid marimba music
and some with clouds of marijuana that led us
to indulge while listening to local jazz musicians.

Then we grew restless again, sold it all
and returned to community service tasks
in poverty-stricken villages where suffering
is chronic and malnutrition is ubiquitous —
something that mattered much more
than veranda-sitting.

2015 Lake Atitlan

I THANK YOU

I may never know what you have given
up of yourself for fear of crushing
something in me that you love.
I thank you. It is the same for me.

Yet to pursue understanding
is another essence of love.

2010

SOOTHING VOICE

Amid vexing dreams last night,
when anger or fear ushered me
toward a twisting, fruitless path,
I heard your voice, Suzanne.

Calming words whispered to me
and although I was deep in sleep,
your hand soothed my back,
giving welcome peace of mind.

2012

SHACKLES OF PD*

As PD weakens and muddles my voice,
I struggle to speak clearly to you of
my thoughts about PD, its impact on me.
It so muffles or scrambles my words
that I fear you may misunderstand me,
or worse, become depressed.

It is difficult to explore my future under PD
for it is unclear and can be fluid depending
on my pain levels, sleep and response to painkillers.

I remain an optimist but loathe the ever-tightening
shackles, as PD changes me from a robust man
to one racked with back and leg pain, loss of energy
and balance so cockeyed I often cannot walk
cross the room or get up from bed without help.

My muddled, mumble-jabber annoys us both
and complicates our usual loving and paced talk.
Writing notes won't do the job! PD has turned
my penmanship to a strange scrambled Sanskrit
streaming jerkily on the page and shrinking in size.
Being homebound is a prison sentence.

Oh how I long to stroll on a forest trail with you
and speak with a clear voice of things we see.

2021

*Parkinson's Disease

TREASURES

We have no thoughts of meeting after death.
Yet surely we will part from life, one before the other,
leaving one to see and hear each day – each night —
visions of the other and the life we treasured.

My goal is and has always been to find paradise
here on earth, while I'm alive, sentient and sensual.
You, Suzanne, have made my dreams come true
because you are a treasure of kindness and humanity.

2004

EARLY YET STILL STRONG

In the chromatic mist of aging,
I strive to find fresh melody for my words,
yet at 82 I wonder if my search will come
up dry, as brain and body slowly wane.
After my next new notes are polished
will I ever aspire for yet another song?

Do I long for something I should have savored
when I had youthful energy and strength –
but that now can be only be a wistful yearning?

I think not, for when I look into your eyes
that have read my soul these many years,
or touch your hand, my urge to continue
happily searching in that mist rebounds.

I am so happy you love me as I love you,
an enduring love that came early and strong.

2021 Prescott,Az

WHICH IS THE BETTER?

Which is the better?
To comfort my beloved wife
through her passage and then
live a short time alone,
with only myself to care for,
or to depart first in her warm
caring arms leaving her only
memories of our adventures.
I can countenance neither thought
and aspire for the attainment of
a mutual old age crowned by a gentle
embracing sleep in each other's arms.

2000

THE MORE DIFFICULT

I only noticed that you changed
into an older woman because
we took photos in earlier times.

I see you now the same way
as when we met at university,
except when you have pain.

That is the more difficult.

2010

BITTER / SWEET THOUGHTS

The sweetest song of welcome
    is looking into your eyes,
as with warm musical notes you ask:
    "Just hold me for a while."

The bitterest of all farewells
    will be that distant day,
when the reality looms of never again
    hearing your voice.

2003

MY WINTER OF ETERNAL SPRING

Fountains of joy, your smiling eyes
ever sing of our search for beauty
in the altars of reality and honesty;
each day, a new spring.

Although winter has come with cold winds
to strip me leafless as a quaking aspen tree,
and my back and legs grow weaker each day,
your love makes my spirit granite strong.

Your voice soothes as does the song of a dove.
Your movements strong and sure,
I dream of you, my darling — oh, how weak is that word —
from twilight to dawn's first gleaming.

The pains and aches of old age blur my view
yet they proffer a pleasant sense of bliss
to be within the envelope of your tender care.
My joy lies in loving our eternal spring.

2022 Prescott

Chapter 5 – Friends and Reminiscence

FRIENDS AND REMINISCENCE

Small birds, perhaps more than any other animal, must be who they are, ever in a state of reaction to external stimuli in their environment. To learn what it is that a bird must be requires observation and setting aside all assumptions of their capacity to manipulate their surroundings for advantage.

In contrast, **humans forever manipulate the environment with little or no conservation in mind. My measure of an enduring friend is their ability and willingness to set aside the powerful motives of self and/or tribal gain. Such friends have always been those** who simply must be who they are, within a framework of honesty, humanism, conservation, and tolerance for diversity.

I pay tribute to several who are special in my life. Most have happy and fruitful lives, despite the trials of aging. As I enter my eighth decade, and thanks primarily to email and social media, my chest of treasured friends remains quite full. Six, in particular, are still kicking up small storms wherever they may be and with the reader's indulgence I will introduce this chapter by briefly toasting each.

Patrick — retired attorney, ostrich-farm owner, with a cat's curiosity and a brain that can absorb it all – physics, culture, law, farming, mechanics, art, philosophy, law, science. He retired to study ethics and Zen Buddhism and now lives, as might a hermit, in an alpine forest meditating on metaphysics.

Armando – Guatemalan agronomist dedicated to fighting epidemic malnutrition in his county. He works tirelessly and elbow-to-elbow with villagers helping them establish low-cost "nutrition gardens" and raise small animals to improve family nutrition, as well as teaching about nutrition and how to avoid transmission of pathogens in home food preparation.

Bruce — a most honest research partner who taught me to "Take it easy," a gift that keeps on giving. Complex in his social and political views, his fresh thinking has bent my own into better balance.

Terry — a St. Louis-born altar boy turned Udall liberal, then a Washington lobbyist and now a respected columnist, proffering solid political commentary in clear prose to an attentive audience. We have changed each other in recent years through sharing our love of common sense and poetry.

PJ — jazz afficionado and drummer, journalist, pool shark, and a no-nonsense Fargo North Dakotan to whom clear thinking, justice and equality are everything. Also, my best after-work drinking, philosophizing and talking amigo.

Linda – my sister, my somewhat younger sister, is the only person other than my wife who loves me as I am.

Several cherished friends have passed — disappeared from my immediate world or lost their way — but they are not forgotten. At least not by me.

SADLY FREE

As our paths split
to separate roads going
who knows where,

we will pursue lives
no more visible to me now
than are the winds.

Distanced from friends
I may never see again,
I feel sadly free and alone.

1967
Upon finishing graduate school

ON MAKING / LOSING FRIENDS

From early on, I sought to make friends
with forward-looking thinkers whose deaths,
I hoped, would be a long time in coming.

Some flowered on my horizon in bizarre
variety like high summer wildflowers, while
others matured to trees erupting with fruit.

I now seek friendships with younger people
because old friends, once brilliant fireworks,
fade, die, or hit "delete," never to return.

Never to return! I mourn those gone without
sharing thoughts about what in their lives
gave them comfort and satisfaction.

1998

REMEMBERING JAY

Jay, always quick to smile and laugh,
funny, creative, loveable, decent; an
idealistic wanderer, risk-taker, natural
defender of justice and fairness.
I remember marching together for
civil rights and to ban the atomic bomb.

I wondered why you fell silent,
not returning my calls. I always enjoyed
hearing you answer the phone in your
matter-of-fact "What's up" style –
your voice so unique and crisp.
I feared I might have offended you
in some careless way or that your
silence traced to illness or worse.

Wife Paula finally returned my calls
to say, so quietly and timidly: *I fear ...*
no one told you, Jay took his life.
I was stunned, again. Jay is my second
close friend whose spirit fled by suicide.

Jay taught me the mechanics of photography,
and to see people up close and personal.
I miss his funny shrill laugh and think of
of the expedition we made into the deserts
of Mexico with his joyous poodle "Boobie."
I ache to talk again with him in the
easy philanthropy of our long friendship.

I feel grief and guilt that he must have
needed a buoy, and I was not there.

As Jay's frustrations closed in, being dead
must have looked more inviting than once supposed.
Did his dreams of how he wanted his life to be
fall so short that anger lead him to conclude
that a quick end would be a better end?

2014

ALONG THE ROAD

There is no need to hoist cups of wine
to new friendships made here.
So many are forged along the road
that we would soon be drunk.
Handshakes will do nicely.
Besides, we have no wine.

2004 Baja California Mexico

LEGACY

Gone from us now, I stand
calmed by your afterglow,
the warmth of your unselfishness,
and am cheered by the depth
and steadiness of your positivity.

My mind honors your worldview
and wishes if any gloom lingers
in the minds of others toward your legacy,
that it dissipate as might campfire
smoke in calm night air.
Your life remains a strong beam
of optimism for which I am grateful.

I measure myself against the legacy Leo gave me:
  ... be a fearless friend of secular humanity.
  ... be one who fights injustice and bigotry.
  ... be a soldier against the blindness of moral certitude
  ... be among those who fight the meanness of dogma and
  ... challenge the pointless cruelty of the death penalty.

In Leo, I admired that he encouraged all those he knew to love,
  defend and pursue liberty and equality for all mankind, and
  always to respect the downtrodden.

Leo was a man of kindness.

December 2016

Leo Alfred Sonderegger (1913-2016.) My father-in-law for 51 years and an intellectual and personal friend. We each knew more than the other about different things, so disagreements were few and sharing was an ethic. Leo will always be, at least to me, the most fair-minded person I ever met and the most willing to sacrifice for his family.

LESLIE

Ochre woman sits calm
before a flickering fire,
transfixed in warm light
that whispers secrets up
the rustic chiminea flue.

Facing the wood-fire light,
her thick greying hair pillowed
upon a rainbow shawl, she is
the image of a Sioux matron
mulling generations of wisdom.

Her back half, the shadow woman,
sits silent, facing the night world
that presses strangely close.
She awaits spirit world truths
to feed her willing, energetic soul.

Leslie, our quiet confidant across
a field of lambs and summer-winter
winds, is a nurturer who speaks of
roses, of goldfish in the irrigation,
and her maturing garden of stone.

Half light and half dark woman moves little,
except as her eyes sparkle with the
conversation. A gentle smile appears
as she floats years away to memories
of moments and friends not lost.

In the reservoir of her molten beauty
lies an image more engaging than
a field of giant sunflowers beaming
in the embrace of a summer day,
A friend such as she is treasure.

2002
Leslie Paterson, a kind-hearted dear friend

ELEGY FOR JOHN GABUSI

Time and life seemed a seamless flow
whose direction was imperceptible,
perhaps not moving me or my friends at all.

This dreamy illusion vanished upon the death
of John, a fearless friend of secular
humanity — a man who fought the injustice
of bigotry, the blindness of moral certitude,
and the meanness of partisan dogma.

The comfort of his friendship vanished
when the space he filled in my stream
of life suddenly and inexorably disappeared.

As he faded behind my own small boat,
his hand rose from the water in a vain
effort to cry "Wait for me." Reaching into
empty air, I could but grieve, as I was swept
out of his time, out of his place, out of his world.

The river turns, John's hand is lost from sight
and something demands I look forward.
Like witchcraft, time again becomes seamless.

I weep at the desolation on the river.
I always knew we would all take this path,
but in November I could not have dreamt
my friend John would take it in December.

2006

MANY YEARS LATER

Many years later
I met her again
and so many traces of
her youthful gaiety and wit
remained embodied.
in the crystal tinkling
of the laughter from
her merry heart.
Her devotion to watercolor
painting reveals her
evolution toward
excellence

2001

GLOW OF RENEWAL

My friend, now older in body
than her years might suggest,
has always taken heartfelt interest
in the pains and needs of others
whether she knows them well,
or stumbles across them teetering
alone along life's fickle cliff edges.

So connected is she to her adopted
wards that they reward her with a warm
glow of renewal, as long as they are able.

2005

LOONS CALLING

When the moon is above open desert, I
think of you, my old, once-young friend,
and of Mexican revolutionary songs we sang
and your spirit of equal justice for all men.
Our recent adventure in Peru to climb
to Machu Picchu re-tempered our bond
strong and pure. Although we again must part
too soon and are of different spiritual minds,
the lofty conversations will flow afresh.

What a marvelous future beckons
as we age and speak or write quietly
of things we know and knew, and of things
that remain so singularly mysterious.
As old friends, we beam upon seeing
that each stands tall with clear laughing eyes
and will sigh at another too-soon parting,
under a sunrise, without words.

So lest we ape greying old goats
I too try to dream of mountain clouds
or aspen quaking in a summer breeze.
Let's not startle the old-man dragon from
slumber with blather that spring is gone.
Focus with me on the sweet clover thoughts
of the way justice in the world can grow
and how our different faiths can succor the weak.

2014
For my college chum Mark Winheld, after a reunion in Peru

ODE FOR ROBIN HOLSKE

Bound for a new life, a college chum
with two wildish dogs re-enters my world.
"Just a broken-down jazz musician," he says.
"My hands got a curse – curls my muscles
so I can't reach indispensable keys.
I'm bound for Las Vegas. I'll teach piano,
do gigs if I can, I've done thousands.
I won't work so hard anymore. I write books
now about my dogs and our travels."

A music major, Robin roomed with me at Antioch,
taught me to better understand jazz and
opened my eyes to how Black musicians get screwed
in the land of the free and equal. We "crewed"
on a racing sloop one summer on Long Island Sound
and marched for civil rights in Ohio.
We were, and are, good friends.

We talked by phone and letters for 35 years.
I could feel his liberal views had become dogmatic,
yet entertaining, as had his curmudgeon personality.

At dinner, his dialogue revealed his shining faith in man,
equality, and his resolve to live fully. And of his growing
disdain for plastic and Republicans. His journey West
excited Robin to tell us what offended him on his trip:
traffic in Florida; the absurdity of "dry counties" in Texas
where a man can't get a much-needed drink; an art
museum in Kansas City that was closed when he arrived.

While the waiter is taking our order, he says loudly:
"I never tip waiters who serve food on cold plates,"
and adds: "Waiter, that won't happen to us tonight, will it!"

Yet, it didn't take us long to reach that plateau where
opinions among friends need not be explained or defended.
It's good to visit with my old friend and music man.
My memory of him is brighter now, and I'm glad for it.

Robin passed in 2019 at his home in New Hampshire, his daughters at bedside

MARIAN: AFTER ALL

After all your gentle encouragement and
happy view of mankind

After all your efforts for calm and understanding
within your family

After all your love of old songs and poems
about small animals

How curious is it that we still walk the earth
while your ashes rest silently

in a vase waiting to be mixed
with the ashes of your Leo

and scattered in some lovely place
overlooking a peaceful valley

filled with white-fleeced ewes watching lambs
frolic amid orange wild poppy flowers.

2016

LEFT UNSAID

On sunny days and in moonlit calm
    shadows ever reach back to me,
    sliding into my eyes and mind
    with memory wisps bearing
    past folly to be contemplated.

Are they calling me to introspect,
    perhaps to self-impeach for deeds
    undone, or apologies or encouragements
    unsaid to friends who now,
    or too soon may be dead?

2021

OLD STALLION LOST HIS WAY

Nick was a handsome vigorous champion
of liberal thinking and action. He drew attention for
his charity and warmheartedness that made
him attractive to fellow students and many women.

But in the glow of popularity, he too easily
cast aside friends, believing they could always
be found smiling warmly in their memory of him,
ever willing to open their arms and hearts.

As time aged him into an old stallion
no one was left to whom he could bid hello.
He learned too late that old friends do not
easily or fully forgive being forgotten.

His lovers fled his promiscuous lust and left
him pining for "just a hug" to escape the frightening
solitude that came too early in the dark of night,
and the deepening poverty of alcohol.

His memories drown in nightmares of love
never found nor truly given. He grew unable
to embrace honest forgiveness or self-reform
and in the end he died drunk and alone.

2001

Chapter 6 – CONFUSING DAYS OF COLLEGE OR BUMPS IN THE ROAD

CONFUSING DAYS OF COLLEGE
OR BUMPS IN THE ROAD

I entered higher education at age 19 in pursuit of a PhD in political science. I was disciplined, and earned two of the three degrees I sought before I turned to business, poetry and adventure. After a couple of semesters facing no-nonsense professors and surrounded by bright and motivated students who, although competitive, were also supportive, my confidence grew that I would succeed in my academic pursuits.

More relaxed, I focused some of my attention on cultivating new friendships, started dating, socializing and of course, as is common among under-graduates, consuming quantities of burgers and beer at off-campus student hangouts. I took in all manner of cultural and social experiences new to me, tried my hand at photography and music, got involved in civil rights and anti-nuclear war movements. My academic focus was on history, government, sociology and music. In addition, under Antioch College's work/study program, I enjoyed five, three-month job experiences in distant cities.

These activities crystalized three new personal goals: first, to make friends with those who might become life-long friends; second, to return to Arizona, my much-loved birth state, and third, before doing so, to find and marry a liberal, college-educated woman with a good sense of humor and who enjoys art and sex. I hoped she would also be smarter than me and could tolerate my foibles.

Antioch proved an ideal place to find such a person. It was a five-year program, so I felt no rush. After four years of hot-blooded trials, the woman I sought found me and became, and still is, my life partner. Getting there, however, included trial and error experiences with women along the way, which in retrospect, I call "bumps in the road."

SUMMER EVENING

Sitting as one on a summer deck,
night slinks ever nearer as we watch
the sun settle between pines until
it disappears behind mountain ridges.

A muffled distant storm roams the sky
and our air grows sweeter with faint
odors of approaching rain that calm
our thoughts of vigorous sex.

Gold fades from sunlit clouds,
light winds eddy, then hush their
whispering in pine trees clothed
in the somber robe of night.

Limbs of pine and oak bow
in prayer to ageless but fickle
rain gods to end the drought and
protect them from dreaded fire.

When the wind withdraws,
a cold wet fog gently pushes us
indoors, to fireplace and then to bed
where earlier fantasies come alive.

1961 Donner Pass

PINES OF ROME

Dear, I must off to university for a time
but first gift you this album of lovely music
which always reminds me of our beautiful love.
Ever should our hearts know such harmony.

May each song sing to your heart of my
love and passion and remind you each
day and night of the life we will share
when I return to your arms.

1960

NOT TO BE

My heart was utterly bewitched
by the brains, artistic temperament
and humanity of my first sweetheart.
Lover of life and gay, she embodied
my ideals and youthful dreams.

Her grace and beauty were beyond
my words, her intellect supreme.
But her love was ephemeral. A lie.
When I proposed she said "Yes,"
then stole away – without a tear.

1961 Long Beach

BRINK OF MORN

The brink of morn prompts
buoyant dreams – prods my
unwillingness to waken, until
nudged by sunlight, I roll over.

Erotic waves were lapping the shore
with soft murmurs in my dream,
while as pilgrim I floated to my love
where she dreams by the crooked bay.

It is sweet to imagine her near
my hungry soul, yet I know
that now awake, I must await
another dream to hold her close.

1961 Washington DC

IF YOU ARE WHO

If you are someone other
than who I perceive you to be

and I am behaving toward you
as if you are someone other than
who you think yourself to be

then who am I to you
if you think I will love the
you that is in hiding?

1964 Chicago

CAREFREE UNION

In carefree moments of union
during summer nights too brief,
what standard of self-respect and
integrity remains within me?

If I say I love only you,
what must I say of myself or
of humanity? Is a narrow love,
a love lost on a path lacking diversity?

Yet in you I love all of mankind
what it is, isn't and what it could be.
With you I wish to be creative.
What is a man without such love?

1963 Ohio

NO

My night is uneasy slumber as
the hours pass slowly. She
lies in calm dreams; I, awake
in troubled thought.

Dawn's smooth silk pushes
the veil of night aside to alight
on our bed, revealing the
grace of youth in face and hair.

Gazing at her marble calm,
a tear tries but fails to form
as I wonder if I can ever say
I love you dear and true.

Knowing my answer is
"No" I ponder if she knows
my passion is mere lust.
Will it crush her trust in love?

She might never know my
heart lingers with another
by the crooked bay whose
face I may never see again.

1961 LA

JUST SMOKE

She is mystic smoke rising
from a neglected cigarette.
Lucy needs spark to give her life
yet her fire is self-consuming.
Her smoke rolls and curls,
twists and turns, seeking a perfect
match with form and time.

But in its rise, the smoke thins
then fades to nothing above
its glistening crib where the
remains of the once fire-filled heart
lie as dry and disintegrating ash.
Once lit, she burned to death,
leaving only a touch of stale air

Ohio 1962

WITH LAUGH AND SMILE

With laugh and smile
    I hold my own,
making inventions in my
    speculations
to appease my reasoning
    that this sense
of happiness is not
    self-deception.

Yet she left and I sit here
    alone each night.
I seem unable to banish
    the emotional dread
of unrequited love or to conjure
    fantasies with another woman.
My arms and heart are empty
    as a hobo's bindle.

I will embrace her again someday,
    I am sure that we share love
and I still have time to wait.

This proved to be delusional.

1961

FRESH AIR

Was I just a moony love-sick lad
promising all and dreaming too high?
Were the things we said and did together
more for amusement than love?

Was it love that moved me toward her
now, or was I merely a lonely fellow
ever horny and in hot pursuit of
fresh oxygen and amusing sex?

When she returned to my arms
from her summer in Mexico I was stunned
that she was so driven by doubt and anger.
Sex with her felt like grudge-fucking.

She has flown the coop of youthful innocence —
her seedling has grown into a bristling thistle.
She is in need of far more than I can provide
and I need fresh air free of her silent anger.

1961 LA

A BREEZE STIRRED

You stand in a fallow meadow,
alone under a cloudless sky.

You have become dew on dry grass,
evaporating in the sun.

Bored with my dreams, you say I am a forlorn
song of a distant, floundering whale.

Perhaps, but I am not singing to you
or anyone that you know.

When you scoffed at my ideals, a fresh breeze
stirred my legs to move toward the exit.

1962

TO COQUETTES

Applause!
You seek respect
for cleverness of mind,
but that for which I hope
will be more difficult to find.
No doubt, you are justly right
and I cannot turn your clever head,
for the pleasure of a romantic night.
You would never honor just any bed,
but don't cast admiring glances at me —
for tonight I seek brandy and think not of tea.

1963 Ohio

BLIND, FOOLISH, SAD AND BITTER

Arching, snow-filled winds
jump street curbs, slash naked
trees, the empty streets and me.

In bitter cold night air, I shuffle
home too weary and alone to care
that I am again a bleeding heart.

My boots scrape the icy path
and I curse aloud to no one, leaving
puffs of steam drifting in the air.

Hands in pockets, I lament my
desire for love in this treeless city.
Yet tears never come for me.

My heart, over-stuffed with eager dreams
has burst and cannot be mended.
She won, her mind, heart and thighs closed.

Without warning, she told me where to fly.
Coldly added I should have seen the signs.
Called me a blind fool. So why am I sad?

Rejoice in my new freedom. Salute her
for her warm passion and for casting me aside.
I learned that romance and lust do not equal commitment.

1964 Chicago

"BE A DEAR"

Eye-flirting across a murmuring room,
a stunner I met earlier and now desire,
rises and glides to where I sit in
unmasked expectation.
Smiling warmly, she leans
close to whisper into my ear.

Her scent artificial, but well-crafted
to seduce, arouses my libido.
As her plump breasts fill my view
I want to turn and press her lips
but sit calm, lest I overplay avidity.

In exquisite slow motion her face
comes closer, hair brushes my neck
as I hope for some divine invitation.
Her breathy whisper tingles my eager
ear — until my brain sorts her words:

"I must leave to meet Fred.
Be a dear and say goodbye
to the hosts for me,
won't you please?

1964 Tucson

GOOD THING, TOO

I have enjoyed sex with women whose
intentions I did not know or care to know,
for we were ships passing in the night.

Most were those who brushed
my hand in surreptitious invitation
that had no future beyond lust.

Primitive lust drove such moments and
I sought more until my brain stepped in.
Good thing too, lust knows only one path.

1965 LA